Growing Up Cranberry

Shannon Gray

Illustrated by Anna Murfield

Published by Orange Hat Publishing 2012, 2023
PB ISBN 9781937165277
HC ISBN 9781645387367
Second Edition

OrangeHat
PUBLISHING

www.orangehatpublishing.com

Thank you to all the local businesses, organizations, family, and friends
who donated and offered me support and encouragement.
Without you, this would not have been possible.

Hi, my name is Crandall Cranberry.

My life starts as a flower on a vine,
which grows in a big sandbox called a bog.

As I grow,
I turn from a flower
to a green berry.

My farmers work very hard all year round
to make sure I stay happy and healthy.

It's spring on the marsh.
I am sometimes watered so I don't get too cold.

It's summer on the marsh.
I am watered because I am thirsty.

It's fall on the marsh.
I am sometimes watered so I don't get too cold.

It's winter on the marsh.
My farmers put a big blanket of frozen water on me
so my vines stay healthy for the next year.

My farmers also help to keep
the bugs and weeds away.

They bring in bees mid-summer
to help me grow!

I can pollinate myself, but bees help too.
Bees carry my pollen to other vines
and pollen from other vines to me.

My favorite weather conditions
are warm summer days
and moist summer nights
because they help me grow big.
The cooler nights help me
to change to a red color.

Around September or October, my farmers harvest me.
They put lots of water in my bog.

Then they use a big tractor called a rotary picker
to cut me off my vines.

Next they gather me all together
using a boom, a floating tube
with a chain attached.

The last thing they do is suck me up a tube
on a machine called a berry pump and separate
me from weeds as they shoot me into a big semi truck.

From here I'm taken to a
processing plant and made into
things like cranberry juice
or dried cranberries.

The next year, we do it all again!

Fun Facts about
Cranberries

~ There are over one hundred kinds of cranberries.

~ Cranberries are very healthy; they are full of antioxidants!

~ In 2004 Governor Doyle signed a bill naming the cranberry Wisconsin's official state fruit.

~ Warrens, Wisconsin, is the cranberry capital of Wisconsin.

~ October has been proclaimed National Cranberry Month.

~ The cranberry is only one of three fruits native to North America; the others are concord grapes and blueberries.

~ Early German and Dutch settlers originally called it a "craneberry" because the flower looked like the head and bill of a crane!

~ A good ripe cranberry bounces!

~ Commercial cranberry production began in Berlin, Wisconsin, in about 1860. Edward Sacket from Sack Harbor, New York, came to Berlin to inspect land he purchased through agents. He found seven hundred acres of "bogs" containing large quantities of wild cranberry vines, so he cultivated them!

~ Cranfest is a cranberry festival held in Warrens, Wisconsin, every year during the last full weekend in September. Warrens is filled with booths containing crafts, baked goods, collectables, knick-knacks, various other items, and tons of all things cranberry!

Easy Cranberry Sauce

1 cup water

1 cup sugar

2 cups fresh or frozen cranberries

In a medium saucepan, bring water and sugar to a boil, stirring until the sugar dissolves. Add cranberries and boil rapidly until cranberries begin to pop or split. Continue to stir until all cranberries have popped or split. Add more sugar if needed. You can serve warm or refrigerate and serve chilled.

Enjoy!